Twilight of SOUTHAMPTON'S TRAMS

By Dave Marden

The skeleton of Car 38 awaits further restoration in the docks workshop on 6th May 2013. The Portuguese tram from Lisbon stands behind it. Dave Marden.

IRWELL PRESS Ltd.

Copyright IRWELL PRESS LIMITED
ISBN-978-1-906919-75-7
First published in the United Kingdom in 2015
by Irwell Press Limited, 59A, High Street, Clophill,
Bedfordshire MK45 4BE

Printed by Newnorth Print, Bedford
Tel: 01525 861888
Fax: 01525 862044
www.irwellpress.com

CONTENTS

ACKNOWLEDGEMENTS

The majority of photographs included in this book are from a collection that once belonged to the late John Bailey. It comprised many images taken by A F Cook, John Fairman and John Bailey himself, together with others whose origins are uncertain, plus a list of the photographs giving details of photographers and dates.

The collection is now held by Bert Moody who has kindly consented to them being published. Despite exhaustive enquiries to various tram societies, organisations and publishers, I have been unable to ascertain much information in respect of Mr Cook's identity, other than he was a lecturer at Southampton University, perhaps in engineering. Neither has it been possible to determine if anyone owns the rights to his images. The Kidderminster Railway Museum, which holds John Fairman's archive, has no record of him taking tram photographs in Southampton. There are also a few other images for whom permission has been given for inclusion.

Where known, the photographers have been duly acknowledged but in some cases it has been difficult to determine their sources and if anyone's copyright has been infringed, this is purely accidental, for which I sincerely apologise.

While some of the images in this volume may not always be pin-sharp, many are previously unpublished and show not only the trams themselves but scenes in Southampton now long forgotten; in some cases, the streets themselves have disappeared or changed beyond recognition. They are an important and fascinating record of bygone days of the town and they depict the end of the tram era, therefore they deserve to be seen.

The following publications have been invaluable sources of information:
Southampton Tramways by Martin Petch
100 Years of Southampton Transport by John B Horne
Dave Marden 2015

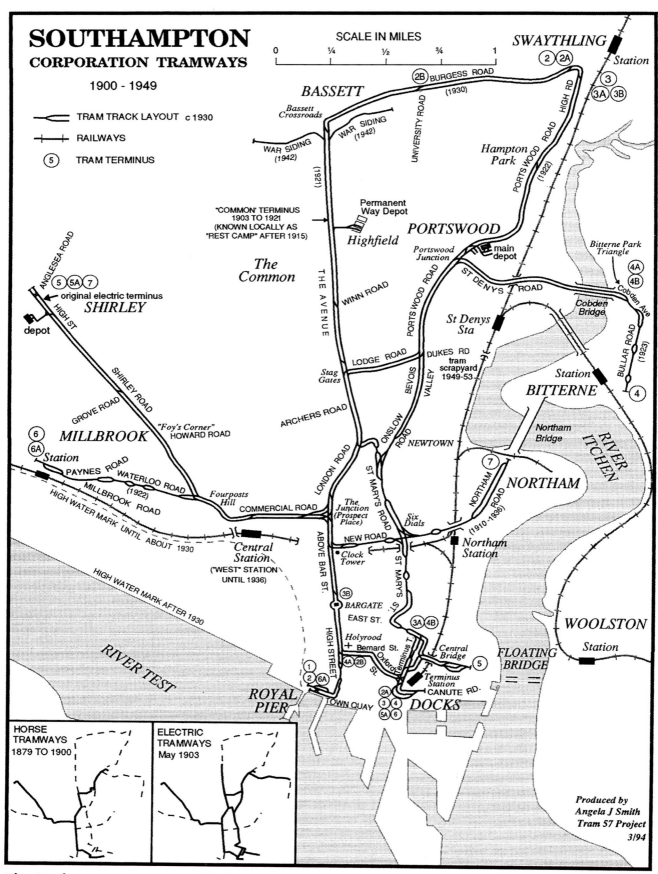

SOUTHAMPTON
CORPORATION TRAMWAYS
1900 - 1949

TRAM TRACK LAYOUT c 1930

RAILWAYS

⑤ TRAM TERMINUS

SCALE IN MILES

0   ¼   ½   ¾   1

SWAYTHLING

② ②A   Station

③
③A ③B

②B BURGESS ROAD
(1930)

BASSETT

Bassett Crossroads

WAR SIDING
(1942)

WAR SIDING
(1942)

UNIVERSITY ROAD

Hampton Park

PORTSWOOD ROAD   HIGH RD

(1921)

(1922)

"COMMON" TERMINUS
1903 TO 1921
(KNOWN LOCALLY AS
"REST CAMP" AFTER 1915)

Permanent
Way Depot

Highfield

PORTSWOOD

*Bitterne Park
Triangle*

④A
④B

Cobden Ave

*The
Common*

*Portswood
Junction*

main
depot

ST DENYS ROAD

THE AVENUE

WINN ROAD

*St Denys
Sta*

*Cobden
Bridge*

BULLAR ROAD
(1923)

ANGLESEA ROAD

⑤ ⑤A ⑦
original electric terminus

SHIRLEY

HIGH ST

depot

PORTSWOOD ROAD

LODGE ROAD

DUKES RD
tram
scrapyard
1949-53

Station

④

BITTERNE

RIVER
ITCHEN

SHIRLEY ROAD

GROVE ROAD

*Stag
Gates*

BEVOIS VALLEY

Station

*Northam
Bridge*

"Foy's Corner"
HOWARD ROAD

ARCHERS ROAD

⑥
⑥A

MILLBROOK

ONSLOW ROAD

NEWTOWN

⑦

NORTHAM

Station

PAYNES ROAD

WATERLOO ROAD
(1922)

MILLBROOK ROAD

HIGH WATER MARK UNTIL ABOUT 1930

*Fourposts
Hill*

COMMERCIAL ROAD

LONDON ROAD

NORTHAM ROAD
(1910-1936)

HIGH WATER MARK AFTER 1930

*Central
Station*
("WEST" STATION
UNTIL 1936)

*The
Junction
(Prospect
Place)*

ST MARY'S ROAD

*Six
Dials*

*Northam
Station*

RIVER TEST

ABOVE BAR ST.

NEW ROAD

• *Clock
Tower*

ST MARY'S ST.

WOOLSTON

Station

③B
BARGATE
EAST ST.

Holyrood
✛ Bernard St.

③A ④B

*Central
Bridge*

FLOATING
BRIDGE

HIGH STREET

④A ②B

⑤

①
② ⑥A

Oxford St.   Terminus T.

②A
③ ④
⑤A ⑥

*Terminus
Station*   CANUTE RD.

ROYAL
PIER

TOWN QUAY

DOCKS

HORSE
TRAMWAYS
1879 TO 1900

ELECTRIC
TRAMWAYS
May 1903

*Produced by
Angela J Smith
Tram 57 Project
3/94*

The Southampton Tram network showing its greatest extent and the areas it served. Angela J. Smith.

Introduction

Although a few of Southampton's trams found new owners, most of those that survived until 1949 met their end at the scrap yard of A F Harris, alongside the railway at St Denys. Among those pictured there are Cars 27, 83, 40 and 85. H.B. Priestley.

I should imagine that only a small and dwindling proportion of Southampton's population will remember its trams as it is now a little over 65 years since the last one to carry passengers ran on 31st December 1949, setting off from the Floating Bridge for Shirley at around 11.00pm. Festooned with lights and amid crowds of onlookers it rattled off into history.

Apart from the excellent *Southampton Tramways* by Martin Petch, published twenty years ago, books about the city's trams are something of a rarity, although many photographs have appeared in various local histories over the decades. For the first half of the 20th century electric trams provided a cheap and efficient, though not necessarily comfortable, way of travelling about. By some accounts, the trams that saw out the final years were noisy, poorly maintained boneshakers and I dare say many townsfolk were glad to see the back of them when the new modern buses took their place. But nostalgia being what it is, the trams are remembered with affection by many, along with others whose only association has been through seeing survivors in a museum or heritage centre. I personally have no recollection of riding in the old trams, but my late mother assured me I travelled on them with her when I was very young, so I have an ambition to be conveyed by them once again.

This book looks back at that final period after the war and, although it is not intended as a history of the tramways, it is useful to have an overview of how they evolved.

Southampton's tram network had begun with horse drawn vehicles on 5th May 1879 with a service running from Stag Gates to Holy Rood and soon many other routes were opened linking most areas of the town. Southampton Corporation took control of the tram services from 30th June 1898 and began electrifying the routes. On 22nd January 1900 the first electric tram service ran from Shirley Terminus to Prospect Place (later called the Junction) after an official opening ceremony.

The trams themselves were a mixture of odd types and individual designs, some new while others were rebuilds, mainly open topped, some of which were gradually enclosed. A glimpse of the future came when the first motor buses ran from the Clock Tower in Above Bar to Winchester Road on 31st July 1919 but the tram era would continue for another 30 years before they were replaced by their diesel driven counterparts. Until 24th April 1932 all traffic passed through the Bargate arch but, from that date, a route was opened around the east side of the ancient monument, with the west side bypassed on 5th June 1938.

The years of World War Two took their toll on the town of Southampton, not least on its tramways, damaged by bombing and with minimal maintenance. Peacetime saw the ageing system emerge in a sorry state. After the post-war period of austerity had eased, there came a transformation of public transport, moving from trams to buses. These were considered more economic with the new breed of vehicles able to operate without the constraints and costs of rails and overhead power lines. The change was inevitable.

What hope is there of seeing trams run in Southampton once more? Many British cities now have the modern rapid transport version, running in single deck articulated units rather than individual cars but their appearance in our City is extremely unlikely, given the narrow and congested streets that make up its main thoroughfares, although perhaps a modern tramway linking the airport, city and the population along the old Fawley branch line might just be feasible?

Realistically, the best we can hope for is for a modest exhibition track running somewhere along the city's redeveloped waterfront, and linked to a heritage museum in that area. At present, based in a workshop in Southampton Docks, a dedicated team is working towards that aim with three trams in various stages of restoration. Two of these are former Southampton vehicles, Cars 11 and 38, and the other is from Lisbon, Portugal. The Southampton Tram Project (formerly Tram 57 Project) has spent many years and countless hours in order to achieve this but, although there is still a long way to go, there is now a faint light at the end of a very long tunnel.

Obviously, the key to achieving that goal is finance and, for my part, I have compiled this book from which all proceeds will go to the restoration fund and I sincerely hope to see the day when the scheme comes to fruition.

Much further advanced is the work on Car 11, looking very much like its old self at the docks workshop on 6th May 2013. Dave Marden.

Chapter 1 - Portswood

Southampton Tramways had two main depots, at Portswood and Shirley, plus a building for maintenance at Highfield. Portswood was the largest of them, and the major hub of operations. Trams entered and left the depot through a cutting opposite Highfield Lane after which various tracks turned off inside the sheds where there were turntables for guiding vehicles into repair shops. Away from the town centre, perhaps Portswood Junction was one of the busiest sections of the tramway system with lines converging from Lodge Road, Bevois Valley, Bitterne Park and Swaythling.

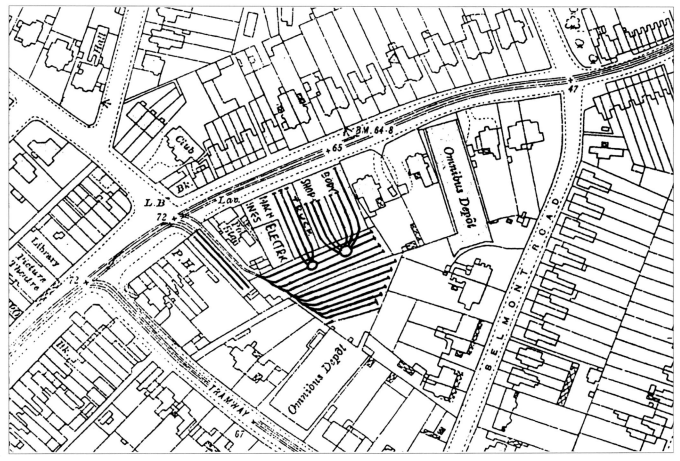

Portswood Junction in 1933 showing the line along Portswood Road running to top right and the one from the Broadway down St Denys Road at bottom left. In the centre is the main tram depot showing the complex system of internal lines and sidings.

A typical scene at the Portswood depot on 30th October 1948 with a variety of vehicles and Cars 2, 27 and 81 in occupation. A.F. Cook.

More trams standing silently at Portswood Depot on 30th October 1948 as Cars 61, 41, 36 and 70 await their turns of duty. A.F. Cook.

Another view inside the Portswood Depot on 30th October 1948 shows Car 66. In front of it is the tail end of the battery powered maintenance tower wagon (see inset) showing part of the tower used to reach overhead lines. A.F. Cook.

Elsewhere in the strangely empty Portswood Depot on 30th October 1948, showing the various roads, inspection pits and two turntables, the nearest leading off to the Body Shop and the one beyond serving the Truck Shop. A.F. Cook.

The passageway leading into Portswood Depot, 24th October 1948, with Car 53 negotiating the entrance and Cars 29, 50 and 104 in line outside. The original horse tram depot was south of the passageway, nearer the camera where the Buy and Hold sign is displayed. A.F. Cook.

The entrance to Portswood depot on 24th October 1948; Car 29 entering, with Car 50 on the left. A.F. Cook.

Car 53 passing through Portswood, opposite St Denys Road with Highfield Lane in the background on 24th October 1948. The front bumper advertises Leicester City at The Dell. The parade of stores features W Gange and Sons Boot Makers, Bennetts Butchers, Alec Bennett Cycles and R C Chaplins Groceries. Out of sight, behind the tram, are E T Moxhams Chemist and Cine Specialist, with Brown and Harrison's Dairy on the corner of Highfield Road. Lloyds Bank is on the right. A.F. Cook.

The driver of Car 77 changes the points at Portswood Junction. On the left is Moxhams Chemist shop with Lloyds bank on the right at the corner of Highfield Lane. W.J. Haynes.

Car 14 passing through Portswood Junction towards Swaythling as a woman passenger alights and makes her way towards Chaplin's grocery store. On the right, a handcart sits outside the Valet Craft premises. W.J. Haynes.

Portswood Junction again as the post-war youths appear to raise some consternation with the crew of Car 40. A Corporation official looks on in the distance. W.J. Haynes.

A pair of trams headed by Car 21 at the top of St Denys Road. Turners the Grocers stands approximately where the Pizza Hut was later situated (latterly Trago Lounge). The photograph was taken on 15th May 1948, the last operating day of Route No 4 to Bitterne Park. J.R. Fairman.

Car 67 heads past the Belmont Hotel (now The Mitre) on its way to St Mary's and the Docks as a prospective customer parks his bicycle outside fishmongers William J Bone. W.J. Haynes.

Burgess Road where Car 50 rounds the curve near the junction with Glen Eyre Road heading towards The Avenue, 6th February 1949. A.F. Cook.

Football specials at Swaythling where a line comprising Cars 100, 25, 17, 30, 51 and 108 wait to take supporters to Archers Road or Stag Gates on their way The Dell, on 26th February 1949. A.F. Cook.

Chapter 2 – Swaythling

Route 1 started at the Royal Pier, ran up The Avenue and then along Burgess Road through to Swaythling. From there it went on to Portswood and then back to the lower town, forming one of the longest journeys on the Southampton tramway system. The Route 2 Terminus was at Swaythling at the eastern end of Burgess Road where it met Swaythling High Road. That route ceased to run past The Avenue junction after March 1949. Trams from the High Road either returned back along Burgess Road or continued as route 3 to Portswood.

A murky 26th February 1949 with Car 22 emerging from the gloom in Burgess Road. A.F. Cook.

Car 21 at Swaythling Terminus on 6th February 1949, ready to set off for the Royal Pier. One of the modern concrete bus shelters has recently been erected by the corporation. A.F. Cook.

The terminus at Burgess Road on 6th February 1949 where Car 21 is about to depart for the Royal Pier. In the right background two of its modern successors await their turn in Swaythling High Road. A.F. Cook.

Portswood Road near Hampton Park with two trams (Car 86 nearest) heading towards Portswood Junction on 24th October 1948. In the right distance is the Newlands pub on the corner of Kitchener Road. The hoarding on the left assures us that 'A little Bovril abounds in the goodness of beef'. The businesses on the left are possibly Baldwins greengrocery, Whitlocks tobacconist and Locks fish and chip shop. A.F. Cook.

Adverts for Cadbury's blended chocolate, Lemon Hart Rum and Drummer Dyes are on display as Car 92 runs along Portswood Road towards the junction, having just passed the Woodmill Laundry on 30th October 1948. J.R. Fairman.

Chapter 3 — Hampton Park

Hampton Park was served by trams operating through Portswood and Swaythling, thus it was part of a long circular route around the north of Southampton. Routes 1 and 3 passed along Portswood Road as they made the long haul back to town.

The section of Portswood Road near Hampton Park, much changed since this picture was taken on 30th October 1948. Car 15 is heading towards Portswood junction as it passes the Vine Inn. On the left is the blacksmiths shop of William Garland White at a time when shoeing horses must have had little more future than the trams. A.F. Cook.

Car 32 in Portswood Road near Hampton Park on a dismal 30th October 1948. A.F. Cook.

Car 100 rumbles over the cobbles of Swaythling High Road passing a tobacconist shop advertising Capstan and Craven A Cigarettes (legendary for their fearsome strength) on 30th October 1948. J.R. Fairman.

Car 106 heading south down The Avenue with little traffic in sight, other than the parked vehicles on the left of the picture, which are possibly outside the Cowherds pub. J.R. Fairman.

By comparison The Avenue at Highfield looks positively busy with two cars and a couple of bicycles jostling for space with Car 105. J.R. Fairman.

Chapter 4 – The Avenue and Highfield

Today, The Avenue is one of the busiest arteries into the city but in the post-war years it seemed almost countrified. The following images clearly show how little traffic there was in the late 1940s. Almost hidden off The Avenue at Highfield was the Permanent Way depot, a couple of sheds that formerly included stables in the horse drawn era. The depot housed maintenance vehicles that ventured out, often at night, for repairs and track cleaning. During the Second World War, around 1942, a couple of sidings were laid to stable trams under the trees of The Common, making them less a target for enemy eyes and thereby insurance against the main car sheds being destroyed.

The Avenue, with Car 44 having just turned from Burgess Road with a group of enthusiasts aboard a special on 29th August 1948. John Bailey.

Standing in the middle of The Avenue would not be such a good idea in today's traffic but the passengers climbing aboard Car 100 near Bassett crossroads indicate how little traffic there was in post-war Southampton. J.R. Fairman.

Relatively 'normal' traffic levels at Avenue Hall on 26th February 1949. J.R. Fairman.

Match days at the Dell meant extra business from the football crowds. Car 25 brings up the rear of a cavalcade in The Avenue including Cars 17, 30, 51, 22, 93 and 108 on 26th February 1949. A.F. Cook.

(Above and below) Two of the works maintenance cars outside the Highfield Depot, with a tour party on 19th May 1946. The vehicle shown above was used for track cleaning while the one below carried out welding and repair duties. W.J. Haynes.

A closer look at the welding vehicle housed in the small Highfield Depot, 2nd February 1949; it was Car 22 before conversion. A.F. Cook.

The two maintenance vehicles under cover at the Highfield Depot on 2nd February 1949. A.F. Cook.

One of the few survivors from the Southampton trams was Car 45, seen here at the Beaulieu Motor Museum in 1960 just before being taken to the tramway museum at Crich in Derbyshire. It is now on display there and occasionally runs visitors on its line.

Car 5 was also spared a one way trip to the scrapyard; here it is in March 1948 at Thornhill where it became a 'meeting room' for the local Boys Club. John Bailey.

Above. Car 108 turns from Lodge Road into The Avenue on 30th October 1948. On the left are the showrooms of Austin dealers Carey & Lambert; on the opposite corner stands the premises of competitors Wadham Brothers. J.R. Fairman.

Middle. An opposite view of the junction as Car 102 passes through Stag Gates into Lodge Road (a wary cyclist dismounts) on 25th October 1948. The former Merchant Navy Hotel (now Travelodge) stands on the site of the building just ahead of the tram. A.F. Cook.

Bottom. Car 21 heading along Lodge Road towards Portswood. J.R. Fairman.

Chapter 5 – Lodge Road

Lodge Road was a useful link between The Avenue and Portswood Road, offering alternative directions for routes 1 and 4.

Top. Not the clearest of images but it does show Wine and Spirit merchants Smeed & Smeed at the corner of Cedar Road as Car 23 as it makes its way up Lodge Road to Stag Gates, 30th October 1948. J.R. Fairman.

Middle. An unidentified car heads along Lodge Road bound for Portswood in the evening sunshine of 25th October 1948. On the left, on the corner of Cedar Road is Edward Rowe's barber shop offering 'Hair Coiffure'. Behind the tram, Williams Grocery shop stands on the corner of Cambridge Road. On the right of the picture is the Pirelli Cable Works Social Club. A.F. Cook.

Bottom. The junction of Lodge Road and Portswood Road sees Cars 104 and 35 pass each other on 30th October 1948. Edward G Robinson and Burt Lancaster were starring at The Empire and you could get a good permanent job if you rejoined the RAF. Whatever happened to Three Bears Porridge Oats and Simonds Ales? J.R. Fairman.

Something out of the ordinary on 26th February 1949; Car 103 has a broken trolley head and is being propelled along Commercial Road by Car 19 on its way to the Shirley Depot at Carlisle Road. A football fixture against Barnsley at the Dell is advertised on the front bumper. The row of shops on the left is now part of history but St Peter's Church in the background remains – though nowadays as a nightclub! A.F. Cook.

Car 89 peers out from the gloom of Shirley Depot on 28th March 1948. John Bailey.

Chapter 6 — Shirley

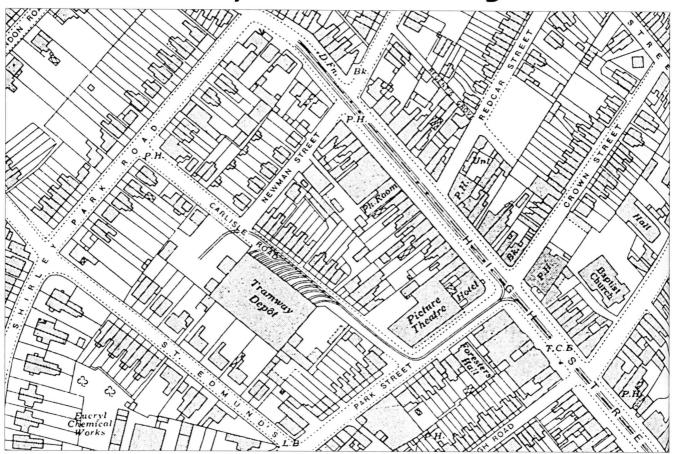

End of the line at Shirley showing the terminus at the end of Shirley High Street and the depot at Carlisle Road, 1933.

Route 5 ran from the Floating Bridge to Shirley and terminated at the top of Shirley High Street near the junction with Shirley Park Road but the depot at Shirley was in nearby Carlisle Road. It was much smaller than that at Portswood but had no less than 15 roads leading into the shed with a siding in the yard for routine maintenance or repair. It was there that several trams were later either broken up or cannibalised for spares while a few examples were spruced up before being sold to the city of Leeds.

Car 38 manoeuvring outside Shirley Depot in May 1948. This vehicle was one of only four to survive into preservation and is currently undergoing restoration.

27

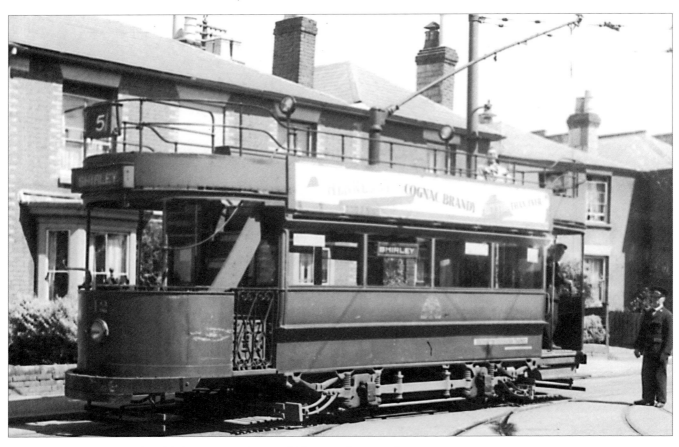

Car 42 arrives outside Shirley Depot in Carlisle Road on 19th May 1946. W.J. Haynes.

Carlisle Road on 19th May 1942, Car 43 standing outside Shirley Depot. W. E. Crawford.

Car 90 rounds the bend as it leaves Shirley Depot along Carlisle Road on a wet 5th May 1942. These open balcony types were unable to pass under the Bargate arch. W.J. Haynes.

More variety in Carlisle Road as Car 50 is about to set off on a special from Shirley Depot, 19th May 1946.

Above. Carlisle Road and the crew of Car 61 pose for the camera on 24th April 1948. John Bailey.

Top right. A number of trams were refurbished at the Shirley Depot prior to being sold to the City of Leeds. Car 50 stands on the yard siding on 10th July 1949, freshly painted in undercoat, ready for its journey northwards to Yorkshire. John Bailey.

Bottom right. Not so fortunate was Car 52; it is being dismantled on the Shirley Depot siding on 28th March 1948. John Bailey.

Above. A sunny day in Millbrook; on 19th May 1946 Car 50, running a special, delivers its passengers outside the premises of Millbrook Shoecraft where proprietor Thomas White carried out his boot and shoe repairs. W.J. Haynes.

Left. Another Special at Millbrook, this time it's Car 37 with a team of camera carrying enthusiasts on 29th August 1948. John Bailey.

Chapter 7 – Millbrook

The end of the line at Millbrook was the terminus of route 6 which ran from the docks via the Junction and Commercial Road. From Fourposts Hill it was mainly single track with passing loops to its end at Millbrook Road, adjacent to the railway station.

Top. **The terminus at Millbrook on 27th October 1948; Car 99 stands ahead of Car 19 and a corporation bus lurks in the distance. A.F. Cook.**

Above. **Millbrook terminus on 27th October 1948, with Millbrook station on the right. Cars 19 and 99 stand in line with a Corporation wartime utility bus in front. A.F. Cook.**

Car 17 makes its way up the slope from Cobden Bridge past Bitterne Park Triangle on 14th May 1948. Note the trees by the clock tower; they were mere saplings then! J.R. Fairman.

A sunny afternoon at the Bitterne Park terminus as Car 32 is about to make way for the approaching Car 12 which will take its place at the end of the line. This was on 14th May 1948, the day before the route closed. J.R. Fairman.

Chapter 8 – Bitterne Park

Route 4 ran from the Docks to Bitterne Park and its terminus was at the southern end of Bullar Road where the track ended adjacent to the Station Hotel pub, presumably a decent place to refresh while waiting for your tram to arrive. The last trams ran to this destination on 15th May 1948.

A passenger boards Car 21, bound for town, on 28th March 1948. The circus is in town, from the hoarding. John Bailey.

Car 96 about to set off from Bullar Road and the dog in the bottom left of the picture obviously knows which direction it is headed. The Station Hotel was then owned by the Courage Brewery, with its landlord's name recorded as H G Ireland over the entrance. This is 1944 and the tram headlight is still covered, for the wartime blackout.

Car 80 runs along a deserted Bullar Road on its approach to the terminus. This was also on 14th May 1948, the penultimate day of the route 4 closure. J.R. Fairman.

Chapter 9 – Town Centre

Obviously, the town centre was the busiest part of Southampton's tram network where most routes converged and ran on to their respective termini. The Junction, also known as Prospect Place in earlier days, where Above Bar met Commercial Road, was always a bustling location. College Place and Bellevue Terrace, off The Avenue and London Road was also a point where trams congregated before heading off to their respective destinations.

The Junction on 26th February 1949 with a convoy of trams on football duty stretching around into Above Bar. Car 83 is nearest the camera; others are Cars 89 and 82 with a glimpse of Car 20 on the left. According to the banner above it, Student Rag Week was in full swing. A.F. Cook.

Apart from the trams and fashions, this scene is still very recognisable today as Cars 86 and 6 pass each other on their respective routes. J.R. Fairman.

The permanent way vehicle has ventured out from Highfield and found its way to the Junction on 16th August 1947. Behind it is the passenger shelter, which has recently been removed for preservation. J.R. Fairman.

Another 'almost familiar' scene as passengers climb aboard outside the Art Gallery in Commercial Road. J.R. Fairman.

A reassuring arm reaches out for a youngster alighting between the tram and a motor car at the Junction. Car 7 is on a short working and will terminate at Holy Rood before returning northbound. W.J. Haynes.

Routes converging at the bottom of The Avenue (top) showing lines along College Place, London Road (left), Bellevue Terrace (centre) and Onslow Road (right) in 1933.

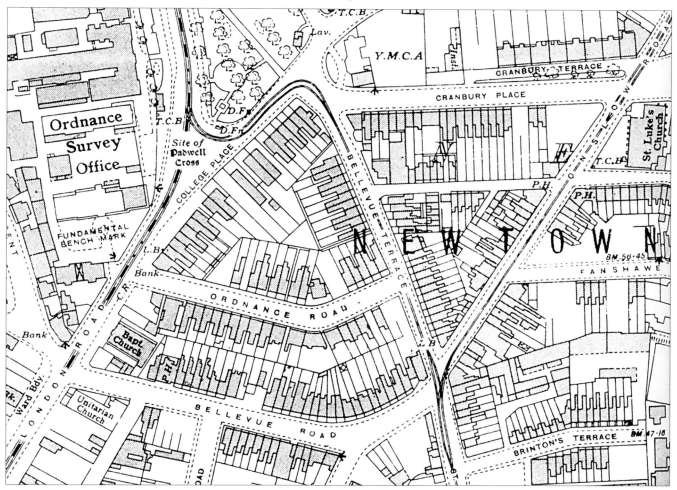

SOUTHAMPTON FOOTBALL CLUB

Top left. Football Cars 12, 108, 93 and 22 await the crowds at College Place on 26th February 1949. A.F. Cook.

Bottom left. More football trams assembled at College Place, again on 26th February 1949, with Cars 6 and 99 in readiness for the returning crowds from the Dell. A.F. Cook.

Below. A final clutch of football fan trams lined up at College Place on 30th October 1948, this time mainly open toppers with Cars 56, 63, 64, and 32 bringing up the rear. You have to hope it stayed dry for the journey home. A.F. Cook.

Car 79, apparently abandoned as the crew enjoy a smoke or a brew, at Bellevue Terrace in March 1948. In the background stands the Newtown Inn on the corner of St Mary's Road and Onslow Road. It later became the Oliver Goldsmith and is now one of many former pubs converted to a convenience store. A.F. Cook.

The Newtown Inn features again in this photo taken at Bellevue Terrace on 8th September 1946 where Car 50 is on a tour carrying Light Railway Transport League enthusiasts, declaring that THE TRAMWAY IS THE MODERN WAY. Alas, it wasn't. A.F. Cook.

Chapter 10 – St Mary's

The area of St Mary's was served by routes 1 and 4 with cars running up and down St Mary Street, and then in a loop around Marsh Lane, Terminus Terrace, Oxford Street and Holy Rood before heading along the High Street. The service through St Mary Street ended on 15th May 1948.

Car 22 at the foot of St Mary's Road about to cross Six Dials and enter St Mary Street on 14th September 1947. On the left stands Day's shoe repairing factory, adjacent to John Day's stationery shop. A.F. Cook.

Car 9 at Six Dials on 14th September 1947, at the railway bridge at the north end of St Mary Street. The Bridge Tavern on the right still stands, but it later became an art gallery and is now converted to flats. A.F. Cook.

Car 25 heads down St Mary Street past Kingsland Square on 14 May 1948. On the right, books are advertised by general dealer D P Mills at shop No.130 but Walt Bonner's boot shop next door appears closed after suffering war damage. J.R. Fairman.

Looking north up St Mary Street in the evening of 13th May 1948. Gouges in the road were caused when Car 78 was derailed on the points in November 1947 while returning from the Docks. On the right, Webber's Restaurant stands on the corner of James Street. Many of the buildings on the left are now gone but the Kingsland Tavern in the centre of the photo is still in business. A.F. Cook.

This section of St Mary Street now forms part of Chapel Road. A tram, possibly Car 23, is passing the Central Hall heading for Marsh Lane on 13th May 1948. On the left is the garage of the South Hants Motor Company, while opposite stands Downey's drapery store on the corner of Cook Street with Day Brothers leather shop on the right. A.F. Cook.

The same stretch of road on 14th May 1948 shows Car 14 passing the Central Hall with St Mary's Church in the background. To the right of the tram is the roof of the now demolished Chantry Hall. J.R. Fairman.

This busy scene shows Car 22 heading along Marsh Lane at its junction with East Street with the tram tracks leading off to St Mary Street on the right. The large store to the right of the tram is that of boot makers William Gange & Sons. The line of shops on the left headed by David Evans the butchers includes stationers Edwin Steel and the confectionery of Edith Martill, while Scott's Restaurant was just beyond the van. All this disappeared with the building of the East Street Centre, now itself demolished. J.R. Fairman.

Another view of Marsh Lane as Car 58 rounds the junction curve into St Mary Street in the afternoon of 14th May 1948. This tram was to be withdrawn form service just two days later. To its right is Martill's confectionery shop and the premises of Mrs Lord, wardrobe dealer. To the left of the picture, on the corners of Threefield Lane, stands Wine and Spirit Merchant R Pera & Co with the Marsh Inn opposite. J.R. Fairman.

Chapter 11 – Lower Town

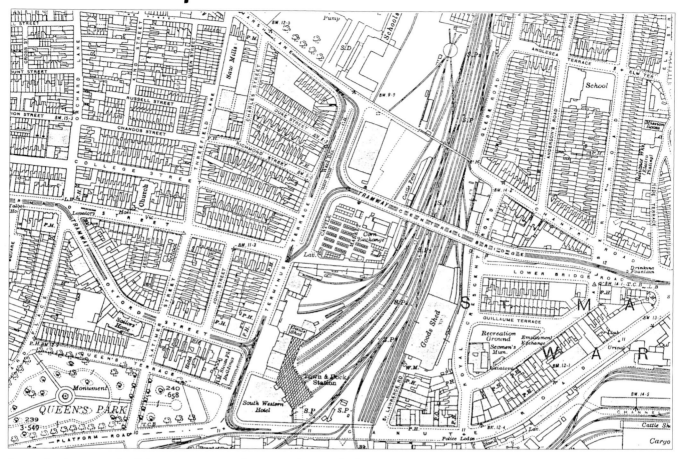

The lower end of the town was close to the docks and thus much damaged by wartime bombing. Services in the area included those around Terminus Terrace and the Central Bridge.

The area around the Terminus Station in 1933, showing the tram routes converging towards the docks terminus at the South Western Hotel (bottom of map). At the top can be seen the line from Marsh Lane where it divides between Terminus Terrace and the Central Bridge. On the left, the line leads off up Oxford Street towards Holy Rood while the Floating Bridge terminus (with its drinking fountain – see also the plan in Chapter 14) is at the far right.

It is around noon on 15th May 1948 at the eastern end of Oxford Street as Cars 12 and 51 head towards the Terminus Station. The shop awnings are those of Miller, Raynor & Haysom, tailors who specialised in military uniforms. On the right is the entrance to the London Hotel. J.R. Fairman.

After the wartime bombing, not many buildings remained in the lower part of the High Street below Holy Rood, as is sadly proved by this photograph. This section of track was interlaced, whereby the up and down lines converged but were not actually joined together. Car 109 heads south past the devastation on its way to the Royal Pier on 5th February 1949. A.F. Cook.

More scenes of wartime destruction as Car 21 passes scarred buildings at the bottom of the High Street along the interlaced track. J.R. Fairman.

The shadows lengthen at teatime along Terminus Terrace on 14th May 1948 as Car 61 heads towards Marsh Lane past Duke street. Directly ahead is the former Deanery School, now replaced by student accommodation blocks. On the right are the steps down from the Central Bridge and opposite these is a store belonging to fruit merchant Fred Trim. J.R. Fairman.

Cars 81 and 6 near the London Hotel, in Terminus Terrace opposite the station, on 15th May 1948. On the extreme right is the Parkers Hotel; many of the buildings in between have been replaced by modern offices. J.R. Fairman.

Left. A rather rumpled Car 94 climbs over Central Bridge bound for Shirley from the Floating Bridge. On the right, at the foot of the bridge, is the Royal Albert Hotel, while to the left of the tram can be seen the old flats in Chantry Road. J.R. Fairman.

Below. Car 50 has featured several times at different locations while running a special for light rail enthusiasts. Here it is again, this time on Central Bridge heading towards Marsh Lane on 8th September 1946. A.F. Cook.

Chapter 12 – Bevois Valley

Bevois Valley has always been a busy thoroughfare, as the main route from the lower town to Portswood. It was a major corridor for public transport where the trams dealt admirably with the challenging slopes of Onslow Road and Bevois Hill.

A fine study of the junction of Onslow Road, St Mary's Road and Bellevue Terrace as Car 17 picks its way through the traffic heading down to Bevois Valley. Ralph Removals is the store on the corner of Bellevue Terrace and the Newtown Inn (now a convenience store) offers beer on draught or in bottles as a smart young mum with feather in hat guides junior to safety on 13th May 1948. A.F. Cook.

Onslow Road near the junction with Cranbury Avenue with Car 93 heading towards St Mary's Road. The poster to the left shows a white elephant with the advice 'If you don't need it – don't buy it – buy National Savings Instead'. J.R. Fairman.

A quiet morning on 15th May 1948 as Car 97 glides down Bevois Hill past the Boots Cash Dispensing Chemist shop on the corner of Forster Road. This building is now the carpet shop Mr H. J.R. Fairman.

Bevois Hill again as Car 94 climbs towards Portswood on 15th May 1948. On the right is Cook's Dyers Shop on the corner of Lodge Road. J.R. Fairman.

Heading west up Onslow Road on 13th May 1948, Car 9 is bound for the Docks and St Mary's. The parade of shops from the right include Sydney Spencer's tobacconist, the Post Office run by Mrs Cox, The Onslow Garage, and Hartley's game butchers. On the left stands the old Bevois Town Methodist Chapel – now a Sikh Temple. A.F. Cook.

Another view of the junction of Bellevue Terrace and Onslow Road, this time much quieter with an unidentified tram squeezing through the traffic towards St Mary's Road. Note the old time emergency telephone pillar on the left of the photo. A block of flats now stands on the site of Ralph Removals store.

Car 100 sets off from the Royal Pier Terminus amid light traffic made up of one car, two distant lorries and a bicycle. Meanwhile, a truck stands outside the Wool House which was then a shipping company warehouse. J.R. Fairman.

It is the 6th March 1948 as Car 18 stands at the pier terminus. Prior to it becoming the town's Maritime Museum, the Wool House on the right was the office and warehouse of Itchen Transport, who later relocated to the adjacent Town Quay. John Bailey.

Chapter 13 – The Royal Pier

There was a terminus at the Royal Pier which, in its time, was an important entertainment venue and a place for families to enjoy the sea air or to take a boat trip around the docks or across to the Isle of Wight. Like many downtown areas it suffered badly from wartime bombing but the pier itself had a slow demise and was finally destroyed by a series of fires.

Cars 22 and 99 side by side at the pier where, on the right, can be seen the workshops of ship builders and repairers Harland & Wolff whose premises were a cornerstone of the docks for many decades. On the left are the remains of one of several warehouses that became victims of the war but the Geddes Warehouse towers over Car 99 and survives to this day as restaurant with apartments above. J.R. Fairman.

The Royal Pier terminus with Car 103 and others along with wartime survivors Geddes Warehouse on the right and the Wool House on the left. W.J. Haynes.

Above. A weary-looking Car 30 stands outside the Wool House at the Royal Pier on 29th December 1948. On the left is the Royal Southern Yacht Club building on the corner of Bugle Street. A.F. Cook.

Left. The sun is shining in this more pleasing picture as the cheerful driver of Car 44 mans his special at the pier on 29th August 1948. The advert on the bumper is for a speedway match against Cradley Heath at the Stadium. John Bailey.

Chapter 14 — The Docks and Floating Bridge

At the Docks Terminus, the line ended outside the South Western Hotel on the corner of Terminus Terrace and Canute Road. Originally, in the days of the horse tram, this track continued along Canute Road to the Floating Bridge but, when the system was converted to electric, it was cut back to the South Western Hotel to avoid crossing the railway tracks that ran into the docks.

The route was then diverted eastwards over Central Bridge down to Bridge Terrace while, to the west, it ran along Oxford Street. Although the Floating Bridge was officially the terminus, the tramway actually stopped short in Bridge Terrace at the junction of Floating Bridge Road and Canute Road. This area formed the southern part of the town's Chapel area which, like its neighbours, suffered badly in

the blitz of 1940 and 1941. Younger readers may ask 'What was the Floating Bridge?' It was, in fact, a chain ferry that carried vehicles and foot passengers across the River Itchen to Woolston and, until the Itchen Bridge was opened in 1977, was the only way to get to Woolston without a long diversion via Northam Bridge.

There were several ferries built for the Itchen crossing. This is Floating Bridge No.9, approaching the town side of the river on 17ᵗʰ November 1951. On the far shore behind it is the Woolston works of the Supermarine factory which played a prominent part of building Spitfire aeroplanes in World War Two. The Floating Bridge ceased operation in 1977 upon completion of the Itchen Bridge. John H. Meredith.

Left. The end of the line for the Docks was outside the South Western Hotel on the corner of Terminus Terrace and Canute Road. Car 82 prepares to depart on 28th March 1948. John Bailey.

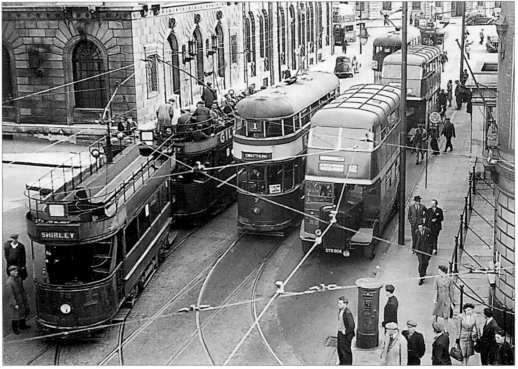

The tram era nears its end as old and new jostle for road space at Terminus Terrace, at the junction with Oxford Street on 28th May 1948. On the left is the entrance to the Terminus Station

Looking almost resplendent, Car 50 stands at the Floating Bridge Terminus with a special about to depart on 19th May 1946. On the left is Chantry Road; the ramshackle building on the right is that of Tagart, Morgan & Cole's sawmill, on the corner of Ryde Terrace.

Bridge Terrace ran from the Central Bridge to the junction of Canute Road and Floating Bridge Road, 28th March 1948. The buildings opposite were once part of Queen's Road which later became an extension of Chantry Road and ran from Ryde terrace to Dock Street. The shops shown to the left of Car 2 were still functioning after the war as Wakes the fishmongers and Percy Kelly's butchers. John Bailey.

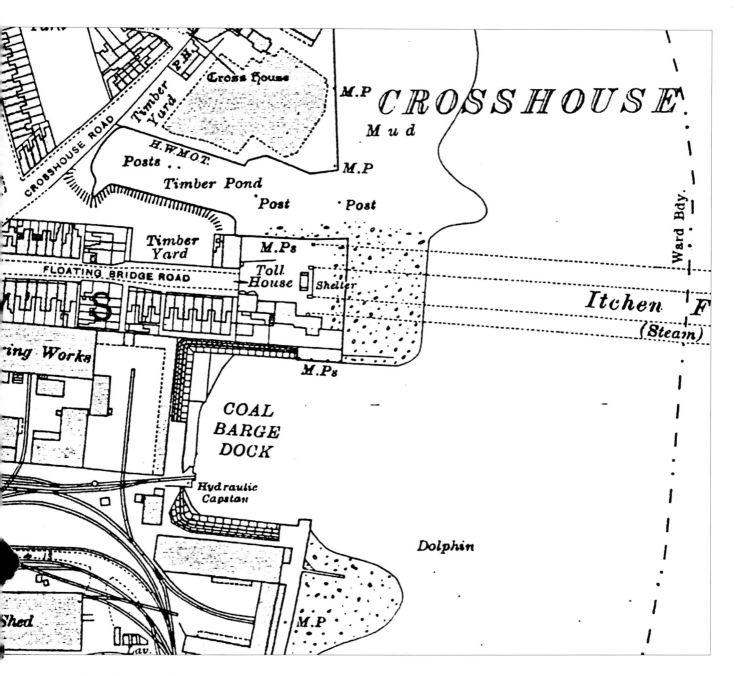

Left. **Car 81 at the Floating Bridge terminus, along with its neighbour, about to depart to Swaythling on 1st June 1947. Just visible through the cab, on the corner of Ryde Terrace, is the newsagents shop of Joseph Reeves-Rowland, still trading amongst the post-war wreckage of the neighbourhood. W.J. Haynes.**

Top left. **A fine summer afternoon on 29th August 1948 as Car 37 prepares to leave on an enthusiasts special. The tall building to the right of the tram once formed part of the Floating Bridge Toll House. Beyond it is the shelter for ferry passengers. John Bailey.**

Above. **A plan of the Floating Bridge area in 1933, showing the tram terminus at the western end of Floating Bridge Road, along with the ferry Toll House and landing points. This area is now largely covered by the Itchen Bridge while the old docks buildings to the south have since made way for Ocean Village.**

The days of the tram are well and truly numbered in this photograph of the Floating Bridge terminus taken on 15th October 1949, of Cars 4 and 9 near the drinking fountain. Staples delicatessen, on the corner of Crosshouse Road, was later a pie shop run by the same family but like most of the area, it was engulfed by the Itchen Bridge construction. However, the building that was the Popular Café on the right still stands, as does the rest of Bridge Terrace. John H. Meredith.

Quite literally the end of an era as Southampton's last passenger carrying tram, Car 9, prepares to depart from the Floating Bridge at 10.57pm on 31st December 1949. The attendant crowd is silhouetted by the blaze of lights as it sets off for Shirley, arriving there just before midnight and fading into history. John H. Meredith.

Southampton Corporation Transport

TRAMWAYS ABANDONMENT

The Route Number will be :

On and after Sunday, 6th March, tramways will be abandoned between Swaythling and Royal Pier via Burgess Road, The Avenue and High Street, and superseded by Motor buses.

15

There will be no alteration in the existing fares.

From Town via The Avenue and Bassett, alternate buses will proceed from Burgess Road into Lilac Road and over the existing No. 10 route.

15

Returning to Town via Stoneham Lane, Portswood and High Street.

11

Alternate buses from Town to Swaythling will proceed via Stoneham Lane over the existing No. 10 route.

11

Thence to Town via Bassett and The Avenue.

15

On the journey to Bassett (No. 15) an " A " with the route number will denote that the bus will proceed through Burgess Road and not over the extended route.

On the journey to Swaythling (11 via High Street and 13 via St. Mary's) an " A " with the route number will denote that the bus will proceed through Burgess Road and not over the extended route.

Fares over the extended route will be :—

Via Bassett and The Avenue

1½d.

Swaythling	..... Bassett Cr. East.
Stoneham Arms	..... Bassett.
Honeysuckle /Daisy Roads.	..... Highfield Road.
University Road	..... Winn Road.

2½d.

Swaythling	..... Winn Road.
Bassett Green Road / Stoneham Lane.	..... Stag Gates.
Stoneham Arms	..... O.S.O.

3½d.

Swaythling	..... East St. /High St.
Bassett Green Road / Stoneham Lane.	..... Pier /Docks.

Via Swaythling and Lodge Road

1½d.

Stoneham Arms.	..... Bowden Lane.
Bassett Green Road / Stoneham Lane.	..... Portswood Junct.

2½d.

Bassett.	..... Bowden Lane.
Stoneham Arms.	..... Cedar Road.
Bassett Green Road / Stoneham Lane.	..... O.S.O.

3½d.

Bassett.	..... O.S.O.
University Road	..... Prospect Place.
Stoneham Arms.	..... Holy Rood.
Bassett Green Road / Stoneham Lane.	..... Pier /Docks.

P. J. BAKER, M.Inst.T.,
General Manager and Engineer.

February, 1949.

The Wessex Press

TRAM SERVICES.				First Car.	Last Car.	Intervals.	
						Early Morn.	Other times.
WEEKDAYS.				A.M.	P.M.	Mins.	Mins.
Shirley—Floating Bridge	...	...	...	5. 5	10.32	10	4
Floating Bridge—Shirley	...	...	...	5.35	10.57	10	4
Swaythling—Pier *via* Bassett		...	...	7.10	10.30	6	8
Pier—Swaythling *via* Bassett		...	...	7.40	11. 0	6	8
Swaythling—Docks *via* Bassett and High St.				5.15	7. 5 A.M.		
SUNDAYS.							
Shirley—Floating Bridge	...	...	...	10. 7	10.32	15	5
Floating Bridge—Shirley	...	...	...	10.39	10.57	15	5
Swaythling—Pier *via* Bassett		...	...	10. 3	10.30	15	6 & 8
Pier—Swaythling *via* Bassett		...	...	10.35	11. 0	15	6 & 8

FLOATING BRIDGE SERVICES.

Weekdays.

6.0 to 6.45 a.m., every 7½ minutes.
7.45 a.m. to 4.45 p.m., every 7½ minutes.
5.45 to 11 p.m., every 7½ minutes.
1 a.m. to 5 a.m., every 30 minutes.

6.45 to 7.45 a.m., every 6 minutes.
4.45 to 5.45 p.m., every 6 minutes.
11 p.m. to 1 a.m., every 15 minutes.
5 a.m. to 6 a.m., every 15 minutes.

Sundays.

6 to 10 a.m., every 15 minutes, remainder of day as above.
The bridges maintain a 24-hour daily service across the river Itchen.